VINTAGE WARBIRDS No 8

1. *Leutnant* Maximilian Mulzer was the fifth fighter pilot to be decorated with the *Ordre Pour le Mérite* when he received this decoration on 8 July 1916 following his eighth victory. Here, in front of a parade of assembled personnel of *Kampfeinsitzer Kommando III* on Douai aerodrome, he is receiving the Military Max-Joseph Order from Crown Prince Rupprecht of Bavaria, 19 September 1916. This award was Bavaria's highest wartime honour and conferred a knighthood on the recipient. See also photograph 76.

VINTAGE WARBIRDS No 8

GERMAN AIR ACES
of World War One

ALEX IMRIE

ARMS AND ARMOUR PRESS

Introduction

First published in Great Britain in 1987 by Arms and Armour Press Ltd., Link House, West Street, Poole, Dorset BH15 1LL.

Distributed in the USA by Sterling Publishing Co. Inc., 2 Park Avenue, New York, NY 10016.

Distributed in Australia by Capricorn Link (Australia) Pty. Ltd., P.O. Box 665, Lane Cove, New South Wales 2066.

British Library Cataloguing in Publication data:
Imrie, Alex
German air aces of World War One – (Vintage warbrids; 8)
1. Germany. Luftwaffe – History
2. World War, 1914–1918 – Aerial operations, German
3. Fighter pilots – Germany – History
I. Title II. Series
940.4'4943 D604

ISBN 0-85368-792-7

Edited and designed by Roger Chesneau; typeset by Typesetters (Birmingham) Ltd., printed and bound in Great Britain by The Bath Press, Avon.

When the aeroplane first went to war it was used for a variety of purposes in support of the armies in the field. Enemy interference with these working aircraft brought about the introduction of armament for their protection, and this need culminated in the appearance of specialist single-seat fighters that were eventually grouped into *Jagdstaffeln*, or fighter squadrons. Pilots endowed with fighting spirit were naturally attracted to this arm of the air service, but strict requirements had to be fulfilled before they could join such an élite band. Generally pilots had to prove their mettle on two-seaters first, and some of the top aces started their victory scores in this way. Unless otherwise stated, the officers mentioned in this compilation served in the Army before transferring to the *Fliegertruppe* and after learning their basic craft almost invariably flew two-seaters before converting to single-seat machines.

The term 'ace', or one who excels at something, is, according to the aviation dictionary, a pilot who has brought down a number of enemy aircraft. The concept originated with the French early in the First World War, and they used five victories as their yardstick. In Germany, the personal mention on an air fighter's name was initially made in the daily war communiqués following the individual's fourth confirmed victory. Additional victories were also reported, and it was thus made possible for the public to follow the fortunes of these 'Knights of the Air'.

The *Ordre Pour le Mérite* was Germany's highest military decoration for bravery or meritorious service in the First World War and had its origin in 1740 when introduced by Friedrich II. It was not awarded posthumously and was for commissioned rank only. The decoration was initially given for eight confirmed victories (e.g. Boelcke and Immelmann), but as the pace of aerial operations intensified it was necessary for fighter pilots to have an ever increasing victory score in order to be recommended for the award, and by the end of hostilities 30 confirmed victories were required. Victory claims were most carefully evaluated, and it was essential to provide a number of eye-witnesses before confirmation was granted. All totals given in the captions are officially confirmed victories; almost all the pilots mentioned claimed a higher total number, but many remained unconfirmed, especially during the last few weeks of the war. Non-commissioned pilots had an equivalent decoration in the *Goldenen Militär-Verdienst Kreuz* (Military Service Cross in Gold), and fighter pilot recipients were usually promoted to officer rank so that the award of the *Ordre Pour le Mérite* naturally followed; thus a number of ex-NCO pilots wore both decorations.

This compendium concerns only the fighter pilots who were decorated with the *Ordre Pour le Mérite*, but of course other fighter pilots who were equally as courageous (but who, for a variety of reasons, never wore the coveted blue and gold insignia) are also worthy of recognition. The photographs are from the author's collection and include some that originated with other First World War aviation enthusiasts among whom particular mention should be made of Peter M. Grosz, Bruno Schmäling, Ed Ferko, Theo Melchers, the late Fritz Schmidt and the late Bill Puglisi.

Alex Imrie

◀2
2. *Rittmeister* (Cavalry Captain) Manfred Freiherr von Richthofen was the highest scoring German fighter pilot and was credited with 80 victories. A strict disciplinarian in the air, he set the very best standards by personal example. He developed the effective use of large fighting formations and from June 1917 was *Kommandeur* of *Jagdgeschwader I*, comprising *Jagdstaffeln 4, 6, 10* and *11*.

3. *Leutnant* Karl
Allmenröder, with his
Albatros DIII. A brave
and resourceful air-
fighter, he joined
Jagdstaffel 11 in
November 1916 and
after his first victory his
score mounted rapidly.
It is some measure of his
ability that Manfred von
Richthofen appointed
Allmenröder to deputise
for him and lead the unit
during his absence from
the Front for four weeks
in May–June 1917.
Awarded the *Ordre Pour
le Mérite* on 14 June, he
was shot down and killed
thirteen days later
having scored a total of
30 victories.

4. Allmenröder's first
victory, BE2c 4179 from
No. 16 Squadron RFC
flown by 2/Lt. E. W.
Lindley and 2/Lt. L. V.
Munn, was brought
down south of Roeux on
16 February 1917. The
aircraft's rudder has
already been removed
and the fin would soon
follow, both to decorate
Allmenröder's room in
Chateau Roucourt, the
officers' quarters at
Jagdstaffel 11.

▲ 3   ▼ 4

5. *Oberleutnant* Ernst Freiherr von Althaus in his Fokker EI, late 1915. After a short spell on two-seaters with *Feldfliegerabteilung 23*, he flew single-seaters from their introduction and operated with various *Kampfeinsitzer Kommandos*. Decorated with the *Ordre Pour le Mérite* on 21 July 1916 following his eighth victory, he was finally credited with ten victories.

6. By mid-1916 the 'E' monoplane fighters were being replaced by biplanes, and von Althaus is seen here with *Leutnant* Neumann flanked by his mechanics in front of his Halberstadt DII. After service in *Jagdstaffel 4* (which emerged from *Kampfeinsitzer Kommando Vaux*) and *Jagdstaffel 14* he was given the command of *Jagdstaffel 10*, but was compelled to give up flying because of his deteriorating eyesight. He was captured by American forces on 15 October 1918 with the remnants of his drastically depleted infantry company and after the war he became a practising barrister until afflicted with almost complete blindness. He died in Berlin on 29 November 1946.

5 ▲　6 ▼

7. *Leutnant* Oliver Freiherr von Beaulieu-Marconnay,
Staffelführer of *Jagdstaffel 19*, with his Fokker DVII.
He transferred to the air service in June 1917 and
by the end of the year was flying single-seaters. He
scored his first victory on 28 May 1918 as a member
of *Jagdstaffel 15*, and in September was given the
command of *Jagdstaffel 19*.

8. Flying latterly against French units, von Beaulieu
counted in his victory log a number of heavily armed
two-seaters, an example being this Bregeut 14 (2639)
which he brought down at Ozeraullin on 16
September as his nineteenth victory. On 18 October,
with 26 victories to his credit, he was seriously
wounded by fire from a Fokker DVII from
Jagdstaffel 74 during a combat with French Spads; he
died from his wounds on 26 October, after having
been awarded the *Ordre Pour le Mérite*. Just twenty
years old, he was the youngest recipient of the award.

7 ▶

▼8

9. *Unteroffizier* (Corporal) Paul Bäumer in his Edelweiss-marked Albatros DV, photographed while serving in *Jagdstaffel 5*. Bäumer flew two-seaters in *Fliegerabteilung 7* before taking the single-seater course at Valenciennes in June 1917, and then served in *Jagdstaffel 5* and *Jagdstaffel Boelcke*. As a successful NCO pilot he was awarded the *Goldenen Militär-Verdienst Kreuz* in February 1918 and was promoted to *Leutnant* in April after obtaining 22 victories.

10. Bäumer beside the Pfalz DVIII that he flew in *Jagdstaffel Boelcke*, this probably being the machine in which he was seriously injured in a dusk landing accident at the end of May that kept him from the Front for over three months. When he returned to *Jasta Boelcke* he scored thirteen victories in September, but was himself shot down in flames and jumped by parachute. Bäumer was awarded the *Ordre Pour le Mérite* on 2 November. He survived the war with 43 victories to his credit and was killed near Copenhagen on 15 July 1927 while test-flying the Rohrbach Rofix single-seat fighter built for the Turkish government.

◀10

11. *Leutnant* Otto Bernert, *Staffelführer* of *Jagdstaffel Boelcke*, with his Albatros DIII. Bernert was with *Jagdstaffel 4* from its formation in August 1916, and after scoring seven victories joined *Jagdstaffel Boelcke* in February. By 11 April 1917 he had been credited with nineteen victories and on 24 April he brought down five British machines in a space of twenty minutes. Already recommended for the *Ordre Pour le Mérite*, he received it on 25 April.

12. In May Bernert was given the command of *Jasta 6*, and he is shown here with a Sopwith Pup (B1721) from No. 54 Squadron RFC which was brought down by a member of his unit; the British aircraft was one of three Pups being flown at the Front in German markings at this time. With 27 victories, Bernert returned to *Jagdstaffel Boelcke* as *Staffelführer* in June, but owing to illness was sent home to Germany in August. He was promoted to *Oberleutnant* but did not return to the Front and died of influenza on 18 October 1918.

▲11 ▼12

13. *Oberleutnant* Hans Berr (right) conferring with Boelcke while consulting a map at Jametz aerodrome. During the Battle of Verdun he led a non-permanent group of Fokker E monoplanes from Avillers aerodrome, gaining two victories. Given the command of *Jagdstaffel 5* (as the *Fokkerstaffel Avillers* became known), Berr took his unit to the Somme in September and was immediately involved in fierce air fighting. He was awarded the *Ordre Pour le Mérite* on 4 December following his tenth victory.

14. A group of pupils and instructors at *Jagdstaffelschule Valenciennes*. Berr (fourth from the left) was in charge of this unit for two months and returned to operational flying in February 1917. He did not score again, and was killed in a collision with one of his men (*Vizefeldwebel* Hoppe) on 6 April near Noyelles during air combat against FE2ds of No.57 Squadron RFC.

13▲

14▼

▲15 ▼16

15. With the emergence of armed fighting aircraft, one approach favoured the large twin-engined *Kampfflugzeug* with up to three machine guns for its four-man crew. *Leutnant* Rudolf Berthold, a pilot serving in *Feldfliegerabteilung 23*, was allocated such a machine and is seen here at the controls of his AEG GII (26/15) while his gunners practise bringing their guns to bear on an imaginary target.

16. *Hauptmann* (Captain) Berthold, *Kommandeur* of *Jagdgeschwader II*, with his red and blue painted Fokker DVII marked with his winged sword personal insignia. Berthold flew Fokker and Pfalz E monoplanes from late 1915 and, following his eighth victory, was awarded the *Ordre Pour le Mérite* on 12 October 1916. A fanatical fighter who did not allow wounds or crash injuries to prevent him from carrying out his duties as *Staffelführer* of *Jagdstaffeln 14, 18* and *15*, he had to be forcibly removed from the Front following severe injuries received on 10 August 1918 when his Fokker DVII crashed after a mid-air collision with his 44th victory. After the war he formed his own corps of freedom fighters, and after serving with distinction on Germany's eastern borders was murdered by communist revolutionaries near Hamburg on 15 March 1920.

17. *Leutnant* Walter Blume, *Staffelführer* of *Jagdstaffel 9*, with his Fokker DVII. Joining *Jagdstaffel 26* in January 1917 Blume was severely wounded after obtaining six victories and on recovery became *Staffelführer* of *Jagdstaffel 9* in March 1918. He was awarded the *Ordre Pour le Mérite* on 30 September and survived the war with 28 victories. Blume was one of the first glider pilots on the Wasserkuppe in the immediate postwar period and was active for over twenty years in the German aircraft industry as a designer with Albatros and Arado. He died on 27 May 1964.

18. *Leutnant* Erwin Böhme (left) and his observer, *Leutnant* Lademacher, pose with their dragon-decorated Albatros CIII two-seater (766/16) in *Kampfstaffel 10, Kampfgeschwader II*, at Kowel on the Eastern Front, summer 1916. Böhme was selected by Boelcke to join him in *Jagdstaffel 2* on the Somme and the two became close friends, but the cruel hand of fate decreed that a mid-air collision between their Albatros single-seaters during an air fight on 28 October 1916 would cause the death of the *Jasta* leader.

17▲

18▼

19. With twelve victories to his credit, Böhme was wounded in February 1917, and following recovery he was attached to the *Jagdstaffelschule* at Valenciennes as a fighting instructor before being given the command of *Jagdstaffel 29*. He returned to his beloved *Jagdstaffel Boelcke* as *Staffelführer* in August and with an increasing number of successful combats was awarded the *Ordre Pour le Mérite* on 24 November. Credited with 24 victories, he was killed five days later when he was shot down in flames by the crew of an Armstrong Whitworth two-seater from No. 10 Squadron RFC.

20. *Leutnant* Oswald Boelcke of *Feldfliegerabteilung 62* flew Fokker E monoplanes from July 1915 and was awarded the *Ordre Pour le Mérite* on 12 January 1916 following his eighth victory. He used his experience to formulate basic rules for air fighting that assured adherents of success and was responsible not only for the formation of the first permanent single-seater fighter units, but more importantly for the strict in-flight discipline that was necessary to make them effective. He is seen here on Bertincourt aerodrome with his Fokker DIII (352/16), the machine that he flew on 2 September 1916 to score his twentieth victory (which was the first for his newly formed *Jagdstaffel 2*).

21. *Hauptmann* Oswald Boelcke, dressed in flying kit and about to fly his Albatros DII; note the leader's wing-tip streamers. Boelcke was killed on this machine (386/16), which was one of the first of its type to reach the Front.

22. This photograph was taken by *Leutnant* Böhme and shows Boelcke conversing with *Leutnant* Höhne in the cockpit of 2/Lt. J. V. Bowring's DH2 (7873), of No. 24 Squadron RFC, which was brought down by Boelcke on 14 September 1916 as his 24th victory. The interested bystander at right is *Leutnant* Manfred Freiherr von Richthofen, yet to achieve a victory. It was in an air fight against DH2 aircraft of the same squadron that Böhme and Boelcke collided on 28 October. Boelcke's machine, with a damaged left wing, was seen to glide away from the fight but later crashed out of control, killing its pilot. An irreplaceable loss, Boelcke was credited with 40 victories, and on 12 December the *Kaiser* decreed that henceforth the unit would be known as *Jagdstaffel Boelcke*.

▲19 ▼20

▲ 23   ▼ 24

23. *Oberleutnant* Oskar Freiherr von Boenigk, seen here in his Pfalz DIII marked with the black spiral band unit marking of *Jagdstaffel 4*, flew initially as an observer in *Kampfstaffeln 19* and *32* before learning to fly in April 1917. After gaining five victories in *Jagdstaffel 4* he was given the command of *Jagdstaffel 21* in October and became the *Kommandeur* of *Jagdgeschwader II* in August 1918. He was awarded the *Ordre Pour le Mérite* on 25 October and survived the war with 27 victories. He died on 30 January 1946.

24. *Oberleutnant* Karl Bolle, *Staffelführer* of *Jagdstaffel Boelcke* from March 1918, with his Fokker DVII, its fuselage marked in the colours of his old regiment (Kürassier von Seydlitz No. 7). After recovery from wounds received in October 1916 while flying two-seaters in *Kampfstaffel 23*, Bolle served in *Jagdstaffel 28*, gaining five victories. Awarded the *Ordre Pour le Mérite* on 28 August 1918, he was finally credited with 36 victories.

25. Bolle (second from left) with some of his pilots on the aerodrome with a backcloth of tents and Fokker DVIIs. He led *Jagdstaffel Boelcke* with such success that this fine fighting unit was able to log 336 victories during its existence, he himself recording the last unit victory, a Sopwith Snipe, on 4 November. After the war Bolle was active in the organization of clandestine training of pilots for the new *Luftwaffe* under the guise of civil air transport. He died in Berlin on 9 October 1955.

26. This Spad 7 from the French unit *Escadrille SPA 31* was brought down by *Leutnant* Heinich Bongartz on 6 April 1917; it was his first victory, and the third of his recently formed unit, *Jagdstaffel 36*. By December he had obtained 25 victories and was given the command of *Jasta 36*.

▲ 27

27. Bongartz, *Staffelführer* of *Jagdstaffel 36* (and third from the left in this photograph) was ordered to attend a trooping ceremony on 23 December 1917 and was personally presented with the *Ordre Pour le Mérite* from the hands of the *Kaiser*. He was wounded several times during his service, and on 29 April 1918 received severe injuries to the head, causing the loss of his left eye, but he managed to land his Fokker triplane successfully near Kemmel Hill. After recovery he was with the aviation test establishment at Berlin-Adlershof and, credited with 34 victories, he died in Rheinberg on 23 January 1946.

28. *Leutnant* Julius Buckler, *Staffelführer* of *Jagdstaffel 17* and seen here with his Albatros DVa, was wounded five times and thus qualified to wear the *Goldenen Verwundete Abzeichen.* As a *Vizefeldwebel* (sergeant-major) he received the *Goldenen Militär-Verdienst Kreuz* on 12 November 1917 following his twentieth victory. Commissioned into *Fliegerbattalion Nr. I*, he received the *Ordre Pour le Mérite* on 4 December and was one of five German aces to hold both decorations. He survived the war with 35 victories and died in Berlin on 23 May 1960.

▼ 28

29. The wreckage of BE2c 2017 from No. 13 Squadron RFC, crewed by Captain C. H. Marks (pilot) and 2/Lt W. Lawrence (observer, and also brother of Lawrence of Arabia), brought down by *Leutnant* Buddecke on 23 October 1915. This was Buddecke's third victory before he was sent with a military mission to Turkey for seven months, and further victories at Gallipoli brought him the award of the *Ordre Pour le Mérite* on 14 April 1916.

30. *Oberleutnant* Hans Joachim Buddecke in the cockpit of his Halberstadt DV when *Staffelführer* of *Jagdstaffel 4*, late 1916.

Buddecke learned to fly in the USA by purchasing a Nieuport monoplane, and returned to Germany on the outbreak of war. He quickly qualified as a military pilot and flew the first Fokker E monoplane assigned to *Feldfliegerabteilung 23*. He was recalled from Turkey early in August 1916 and gained four victories in September, but spent almost the whole of 1917 on a second Turkish detachment. He was credited with thirteen victories when he was killed in action as a member of *Jagdstaffel 18* on 10 March 1918.

31. *Leutnant* Franz Büchner, *Staffelführer* of *Jagdstaffel 13*, with his mechanics and decorated Fokker DVII, September 1918. The photograph was taken following Büchner's 30th victory on 18 September, when he was recommended for the *Ordre Pour le Mérite*, but such was the pace of his successful combats that by the time officialdom had caught up and made the award on 25 October Büchner had achieved 40 victories, all but one in the previous twelve months. The original photograph was suitably adorned by marking the space in the centre of the laurel wreath with his victory total.

32. Despite the discouraging start to his air fighting career when he served six months in *Jagdstaffel 9* from March 1917 without success (except for a contested claim in August 1917 that was eventually confirmed), Büchner never lost his offensive spirit and developed into a fine fighter pilot. After the war he remained in military service flying for the *Reichswehr*, but was shot down and killed over Leipzig on 18 March 1920 during the fighting that accom-panied the communist unrest in that city.

33. *Leutnant* Walter von Bülow served in *Feldfliegerabteilung 22* and scored two victories in October 1915, although whether these victories were obtained on a single-seat E monoplane or on this twin-engined AEG GII (19/15) which was successfully used for air fighting by the unit is not known. Before joining the newly formed *Jagdstaffel 18* in December 1916 von Bülow served in Palestine with *Feldfliegerabteilung 300*.

34. FE2d A5149, from No. 20 Squadron RFC, flown by Lt. A. W. Martin with Pte. W. C. Blake as gunner, was brought down on *Jagdstaffel 18*'s aerodrome at Menin on 7 May 1917 by von Bülow as his thirteenth victory. The aircraft was repaired and flown by the Germans for a period. Given the command of *Jagdstaffel 36* in May, Walter von Bülow was awarded the *Ordre Pour le Mérite* on 8 October following his 21st victory and was posted to *Jagdstaffel Boelcke* as *Staffelführer* in December, but he was shot down and killed on 6 January 1918 having accumulated 28 victories.

33▲   34▼

35. After a number of years in the merchant service, *Oberleutnant* Friedrich Christiansen (seen here cocking the forward gun of his Brandenberg W12 seaplane) learned to fly in 1914 at the age of 34, and flew seaplanes from Zeebrugge from January 1915, becoming Station Commander in September 1917. When he was awarded the *Ordre Pour le Mérite* on 12 December he had carried out 440 operational flights totalling 1,164 hours. Credited with 27 victories, he survived the war and held high office in the National Socialist Flying Corps (NSFK) in the 1930s. He was promoted to *General der Flieger* (Air Marshal), and became military governor of occupied Holland during the Second World War, the postwar retribution for which was a period of imprisonment. He died on 3 December 1972.

36. Action in the North Sea. Not all of Christiansen's activities concerned enemy aircraft: here his Brandenberg W12 seaplane (1183), bearing his personal marking of a 'C' in a diamond on a white band on the rear fuselage, is seen over the burning Dutch schooner *Meeuw* on 21 April 1918. The ship, loaded with contraband, was stopped in a prohibited area and was eventually set alight by machine-gun fire.

37. *Leutnant* Karl Degelow, *Staffelführer* of *Jagdstaffel 40*, with his Fokker DVII; the aircraft shows his personal marking, a leaping white stag. Degelow scored his first victory in May 1917 while flying two-seaters in *Fliegerabteilung (A) 216*, and following conversion to single-seaters at *Jagdstaffelschule I* at Valenciennes was posted to *Jagdstaffel 7*. He gained four victories before being transferred to *Jagdstaffel 40*, becoming *Staffelführer* of that unit in July 1918. He was decorated with the *Ordre Pour le Mérite* (as the last recipient of the award) on 9 November and was credited with 30 victories. Degelow served in the *Luftwaffe* during the Second World War and attained the rank of *Major*. He died in Hamburg on 9 November 1970.

38. *Leutnant* Albert Dossenbach (left) with his observer *Oberleutnant* Hans Schilling, a two-seater crew of *Feldfliegerabteilung 22* that fought many successful air combats in the latter half of 1916. Both men are wearing the Knight's Cross of the House Order of Hohenzollern awarded to them on 21 October 1916; this was the usual preliminary to the award of the *Ordre Pour le Mérite*.

37 ▲   38 ▼

39. Dossenbach was awarded the *Ordre Pour le Mérite* on 11 November 1916 following his eighth victory. Given the command of *Jagdstaffel 36* on its formation in February 1917, he obtained five victories in April but was wounded by bomb splinters when about to take off to attack French aircraft which were bombing the aerodrome. He returned to the Front as *Staffelführer* of *Jagdstaffel 10* in June but was shot down and killed in a fight with two Bristol Fighters on 3 July. He was credited with fifteen victories.

40. *Leutnant* Eduard Dostler (right) watches while his observer, *Leutnant* Boes, explains the defects of his Parabellum machine gun to *Waffenmeister* Latzinger, the mechanic responsible for the armament of Dostler's LFG Roland CII *Walfisch* in *Kampfstaffel 36*. The destruction of a Nieuport Scout by this crew on 17 December 1916 was the first of Dostler's 26 victories. Ten days later he was appointed *Staffelführer* of *Jagdstaffel 13* and in February 1917 moved to *Jagdstaffel 34* in the same capacity.

39 ▶

▼ 40

41▲

41. Dostler became the *Staffelführer* of *Jasta* 6 in June 1917, and with 21 victories was awarded the *Ordre Pour le Mérite* on 6 August. When the news came through Manfred von Richthofen (with bandaged head from his wound on 6 July) loaned Dostler his own decoration so that the latter could be photographed wearing the award. Shot down and killed fourteen days later, Dostler was credited with 26 victories.

42. Wilhelm Frankl learned to fly before the war and scored his first victory on 10 May 1915 when he brought down a French Voisin with a five-shot carabine as a *Vizefeldwebel* in *Feldfliegerabteilung 40*. He flew Fokker E monoplanes in his unit and with *Kampfeinsitzer Kommando Vaux*; he was promoted to *Leutnant* in May 1916, and he was awarded the *Ordre Pour le Mérite* on 12 August following his eighth victory.

◀42

▲ 43

▲ 44   ▼ 45

43. Frankl has an admiring audience as he poses with the wreckage of a French Nieuport 17 (1442). He was credited with eleven victories in *Jagdstaffel 4*, including four British aircraft on 6 April 1917, one of which was FE2b 7714 from No. 100 Squadron RFC crewed by 2/Lt Richards and 2AM Barnes at 02.30am (German time) – probably the first night-fighter victory in history. Frankl was killed two days later when his Albatros DIII broke up in the air following combat with a Bristol Fighter. He had nineteen victories to his credit.

44. By the end of 1914 *Leutnant* Hermann Göring (left) was flying as *Leutnant* Bruno Loerzer's observer on Albatros BI two-seaters in *Feldfliegerabteilung 25*. He learned to fly at the Aviatik school at Freiburg and was soon flying single-seaters in *Jagdstaffeln 5* and *26* before becoming *Staffelführer* of *Jagdstaffel 27*. Promoted to *Oberleutnant* in August 1917, he was awarded the *Ordre Pour le Mérite* on 2 June 1918 and in July was given the command of *Jagdgeschwader I*.

45. Victor in 22 aerial combats, Göring stands by the white Fokker DVII that he flew late in 1918 as *Kommandeur* of *Jagdgeschwader Freiherr von Richthofen Nr. I*. He is wearing the modified and strengthened harness for the static line-operated Heinecke parachute, an item of equipment used by German fighter pilots from April 1918 onwards. Better known as *Reichsmarschall* of the *Luftwaffe* during the Second World War, he committed suicide in Nürnberg on 15 October 1946.

46. *Leutnant* Heinrich Gontermann with his Albatros DIII and mechanics, photographed while serving in *Jagdstaffel 5*, March 1917. Gontermann undertook his first operational flights on LFG Roland CII *Walfisch* and Ago CI two-seaters in *Kampfstaffel Tergnier* before converting to single-seaters at Cologne and joining *Jagdstaffel 5* in November 1916. Despite the obvious dangers, observation balloons held a strange fascination for him and his final score of 39 victories included the destruction of seventeen balloons.

47. Gontermann with the crew of FE2d A1948 from No. 57 Squadron RFC (2/Lt. F. E. Hills and 2/Lt. A. G. Ryall) on 6 March 1917. The British crew had an amazing escape: brought down in flames, they jumped out of their machine as it touched the ground and before it turned upside down to be completely destroyed. This was Gontermann's second victory; some two months later he was given the command of *Jagdstaffel 15*, and he was awarded the *Ordre Pour le Mérite* on 14 May. He died on 30 October from injuries received in the crash of his Fokker DrI triplane (115/17) caused by the structural failure of its upper wing.

46▲ 47▼

48

48. *Leutnant* Robert Greim (left) with his observer, *Leutnant* Wimmer, in front of their LVG CII in *Feldfliegerabteilung 3b* in 1916. Greim was a prewar professional soldier who scored his first victory when flying as a self-taught observer on 10 October 1915. He learned to fly at Schleissheim and joined *Jagdstaffel 34* in April 1917, and when fighters were being operated in non-permanent assemblies of *Jagdstaffeln* (*Jagdgruppen*) in late 1917 and 1918 he commanded *Jagdgruppe 10*, which was later known as *Jagdgruppe Greim*.

49. *Oberleutnant* Robert Greim, *Staffelführer* of *Jagdstaffel 34b*, with his Albatros DIII, 2108/16, summer 1917. He was awarded the *Ordre Pour le Mérite* on 8 October 1918 and survived the war with 28 victories; he was also credited with the destruction of a British tank. Honoured with the Military Max-Joseph Order on 25 November 1920, Ritter von Greim remained active in aviation and joined the newly formed *Luftwaffe* in 1935, reaching the final rank of *Generalfeld-marschall*. Following the defeat of Germany and shortly after having been taken prisoner, he committed suicide on 24 May 1945.

50. *Leutnant* Walter Höhndorf (right) seen here with *Oberleutnant* Buddecke, was engaged in the design and construction of aircraft with Union-Flugzeugwerke at Teltow near Berlin from prewar days. He served on two-seaters with *Feldfliegerabteilungen 12* and 67 but was periodically returned to Germany for test-flying duties. He flew single-seaters with various *Kampfeinsitzer Kommandos* and was awarded the *Ordre Pour le Mérite* on 20 July 1916 following his eighth victory.

51. Höhndorf's front-line experience and aeronautical technical knowledge caused him to be involved in the design and construction of the AEG DI fighter biplane, which had an all-metal structure. He personally flew this aircraft at the Front, attached to *Jagdstaffel 14*, but was killed in a crash on this machine during a test flight at Ire-le-Sec on 5 September 1917. Höhndorf was credited with twelve victories.

50▲ 51▼

D4400/17
AEG

52. The Eagle of Lille: *Leutnant* Max Immelmann with the wreckage of his seventh victory, Morane Parasol 5087 from No. 3 Squadron RFC, flown by Lt. A. V. Hobbs (pilot) and 2/Lt. C. E. G. Tudor-Jones (observer) and brought down over Valenciennes on 15 December 1915. Immelmann was a two-seater pilot in *Feldfliegerabteilung 62* at Douai who converted to Fokker E monoplanes under instruction from Boelcke at the end of July 1915. During the following months his victory score kept pace with that of Boelcke, both pilots being awarded the *Ordre Pour le Mérite* on 12 January 1916 following their eighth victories.

▲ 52   ▼ 53

53. Promoted to *Oberleutnant* in April 1916, Max Immelmann was leader of *Kampfeinsitzer Kommando III*, a group of German VI Army single-seaters that would later become the nucleus for *Jagdstaffeln 10* and *11*. He is seen here in front of his Fokker EIV with a visiting dignitary to Douai, Crown Prince Boris of Bulgaria. Immelmann, who had fifteen victories, was killed on 18 June 1916 during an air-fight with FE2bs of No. 25 Squadron RFC. Faulty machine gun synchronizer gear caused him to shoot a blade off his own propeller and the resulting severe vibration from the whirling, unbalanced, nine-cylinder rotary engine caused the complete structural failure of his Fokker EIII, which fell in four main pieces into the eastern outskirts of Lens.

54. The instructor shows how! This is the Halberstadt DV crashed by *Leutnant* Josef Jacobs at the *Jagdstaffelschule* in Valenciennes, December 1916. Experienced fighter pilots were attached to the school as fighting instructors and Jacobs, although he only had one victory at the time, had been flying single-seaters for almost twelve months with *Feldfliegerabteilung 11* and *Fokkerstaffel West* when the accident happened.

55. After serving in *Jagdstaffel 22*, Jacobs, now with five victories to his credit, became the *Staffelführer* of *Jagdstaffel 7* in August 1917. He was awarded the *Ordre Pour le Mérite* on 18 July 1918 after his 22nd victory, and went on to achieve a total of 41, many of them obtained on the Fokker triplane. He is seen here (second from left) in October following his 39th victory. Jacobs served in *Kampfgeschwader Sachsenberg* in 1919. He led a varied life postwar and was for a period a successful motor racing driver. He died in Munich on 29 July 1978.

54▲   55▼

56. *Leutnant* Hans Kirschstein, acting *Staffelführer* of *Jagdstaffel 6*, served in *Fliegerabteilung 19* before converting to single-seaters at the *Jagdstaffelschule* in Valenciennes, joining the unit in March 1918. An exceptional pilot and an aggressive fighter, he obtained 27 victories in less than three months and was awarded the *Ordre Pour le Mérite* on 24 June. He died from injuries received in a flying accident to a Hannover two-seater in which he was the passenger on 16 July that year.

57. *Leutnant* Otto Kissenberth, of *Fliegerabteilung 9b*, with his Pfalz EI single-seater. Kissenberth began to take flying instruction before the war, and as a war volunteer rapidly completed his pilot training, joining *Feldfliegerabteilung 8b* in January 1915. Wounded in an early air combat, he undertook many reconnaissance and bombing flights on two-seaters, and he flew single-seaters with *Feldfliegerabteilung 9b* from August 1915, being leader of a non-permanent assembly of single-seaters known as *Kampfeinsitzer Kommando Ensisheim* from December.

58. This Breguet V of the Royal Naval Air Service, crewed by FSL Rockey and GL Sturdee, was one of three Allied aircraft brought down by Kissenberth on 12 October 1916 out of a large formation en route to bomb the Mauser factory at Oberndorf in southern Germany. Kissenberth served in *Jagdstaffel 16* (as the *Ensisheim Kommando* became known) and was given the command of *Jagdstaffel 23* in August 1917. Credited with nineteen victories, he was seriously injured in May 1918 when he crashed in a captured Sopwith Camel. He was awarded the *Ordre Pour le Mérite* on 30 June, was promoted to *Oberleutnant*, and did not return to the Front. Kissenberth was killed whilst mountaineering in the Alps on 2 August 1919.

59. *Leutnant* Hans Klein on a visit to the Pfalz Flugzeugwerke in 1918. During his short tenure as a fighter pilot from April 1917, when he joined *Jagdstaffel 4*, until the end of November, when he was flying as *Staffelführer* of *Jagdstaffel 10*, Klein obtained 22 victories and was awarded the *Ordre Pour le Mérite* on 4 December. He was severely wounded in an air fight in February 1918 and did not return to operational flying, but he joined the *Luftwaffe* as a *Major* in 1935 and held various senior appointments, reaching high rank. He died in 1944.

56 ▶

▼ 57

58 ▲ 59 ▼

▲ 60 ▼ 61

60. *Vizefeldwebel* Otto Könnecke, of *Jagdstaffel 5*, with his mechanics and his Albatros DV, in front of the sheds at Boistrancourt aerodrome. A prewar military pilot who learned to fly at Metz, Könnecke was serving as a flying instructor at the outbreak of war and did not go to the Front until 1916. He joined *Jagdstaffel 25* in Macedonia in December 1916, scored his first victory in February 1917, and was transferred to *Jagdstaffel 5* in April, becoming one of the most successful pilots in the unit.

61. Könnecke was awarded the *Goldenen Militär-Verdienst Kreuz* in May 1918 and by the end of the month had twenty victories. Promoted to *Leutnant*, he was awarded the *Ordre Pour le Mérite* on 26 September and survived the war, having gained 35 victories. Könnecke continued flying after the war and was with Lufthansa from its formation in 1926 before joining the *Luftwaffe* in 1935. He died on 25 January 1956.

62. *Leutnant* Heinrich Kroll, *Staffelführer* of *Jagdstaffel 24*, seen here with his Fokker DVII, served initially in *Jagdstaffel 9*. His third victory was found to be the Spad of France's fourth ranking ace (23 victories), René Dorme. Appointed *Staffelführer* of *Jagdstaffel 24* in June 1917, Kroll was awarded the *Ordre Pour le Mérite* on 29 March 1918 following his 22nd victory. He went on to achieve 30 victories before being seriously wounded on 14 August; he survived the war but died of pneumonia in Hamburg on 21 February 1930.

63. Albatros DV 2214/17 was flown by Kroll in *Jagdstaffel 24*. This aircraft was a lightened version of the popular Albatros DIII, but the attempts made to improve its performance by this means were not successful and the changes robbed the basic design of the ruggedness that had been one of the attributes of the earlier machine. This particular DV was crashed by a unit pilot on 12 October 1917 when, short of fuel, he landed on soft ground and turned upside down.

62 ▲

63 ▼

▲ 64   ▼ 65

64. *Leutnant* Arthur Laumann and the Dutch aircraft designer Anthony Fokker pose beside a Fokker DVII marked with the black and white stripes signifying *Jagdstaffel 6*. A war volunteer, Laumann flew two-seaters in *Fliegerabteilung (A) 265* and joined *Jagdstaffel 66* in May 1918 without undertaking the usual fighter conversion course. With 22 victories to his credit, he was given the command of *Jagdstaffel 10* following the loss of Löwenhardt.

65. *Staffelführer* of *Jagdstaffel 10*, Laumann marked his Fokker DVII with his initials as a personal decoration. He was awarded the *Ordre Pour le Mérite* on 25 October 1918, survived the war with 27 victories, and joined the *Luftwaffe* in 1935. Having served in a component unit of *Jagdgeschwader I*, it was appropriate that he became *Kommandeur* of *II/Jagdgeschwader Freiherr von Richthofen Nr. 132*. He died on 18 November 1970.

66. Unteroffizier Gustav Leffers standing directly under the propeller boss of the 120hp Benz engine of his LVG B two-seater of *Feldfliegerabteilung 32* in February 1915. An outstanding pilot, Leffers was promoted to *Leutnant* in July and flew the first Fokker E monoplane assigned to the unit, scoring two victories in December. During 1916 he was attached to *Kampfeinsitzer Staffel B*, a non-permanent grouping of single-seaters on Bertincourt aerodrome that was expanded and designated *Jagdstaffel 1* in August that year.

67. Leffers with the captured Nieuport 11 that he used in *Jagdstaffel 1*; note that its over-wing Lewis gun has been replaced with an LMG 08/15 synchronized to fire through the propeller. Following his eighth victory, Leffers was awarded the *Ordre Pour le Mérite* on 5 November but was shot down and killed on 27 December, reputedly while flying the Nieuport. He was officially credited with nine victories.

66 ▲   67 ▼

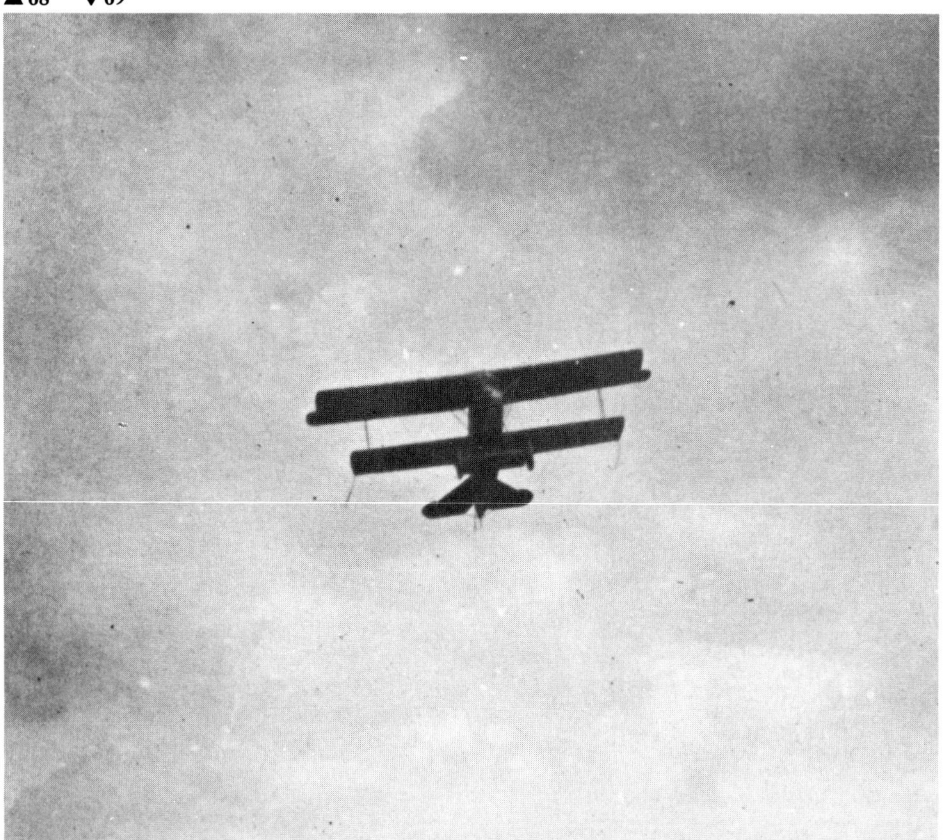

68. *Leutnant* Erich Löwenhardt (right), *Staffelführer* of *Jagdstaffel 10*, with *Leutnant* Friedrichs beside a captured Spad 13. Löwenhardt served at first as an observer, but after being trained as a pilot he flew two-seaters in *Fliegerabteilung (A) 265*, undertook the *Jagdstaffelschule* course and joined *Jasta 10* in March 1917. He became *Staffelführer* of this unit on 10 April 1918 and was awarded the *Ordre Pour le Mérite* on 31 May.

69. Löwenhardt flying his yellow Fokker DVII and displaying leader's streamers. His victory score mounted steadily and included eight observation balloons. He was promoted to *Oberleutnant* on 7 August 1918, and three days later, in the heat of a fierce dog-fight, and even as he shot down an SE5a over Chaulnes as his 54th victory, his machine was rammed by another Fokker DVII. Although he apparently jumped by parachute, the canopy did not develop and he was killed. Löwenhardt was a fine fighter and a skilled leader, and his death was a great loss to *Jagdgeschwader I*.

70. Leutnant Bruno Loerzer (left), from *Feldfliegerabteilung 25*, shows Crown Prince Wilhelm over Fokker EIII 401/15 at Jametz,

20 January 1916. Loerzer was a professional soldier and flew Fokker E monoplanes attached to various formations in the Champagne and at Verdun from July 1915, obtaining his first victories in March 1916. Promoted to *Oberleutnant* in April, he was badly wounded in air combat but after recovery flew with *Kampfstaffel Metz*, which was later designated *Jagdstaffel 17*.

71. *Oberleutnant* Bruno Loerzer, *Staffelführer* of *Jagdstaffel 26* with his Albatros DV (2299/17), striped in the black and white unit marking which was introduced during the summer of 1917. Loerzer was awarded the *Ordre Pour le Mérite* on 21 February 1918 following his 22nd victory and became at this time the *Kommandeur* of *Jagdgeschwader III*, comprising *Jagdstaffeln Boelcke, 26, 27* and *36*. Promoted to *Hauptmann* on 10 October 1918, he survived the war, with 44 victories to his credit. He was active in aviation between the wars and served again in the *Luftwaffe*, reaching high rank. He died on 23 August 1960.

▲72

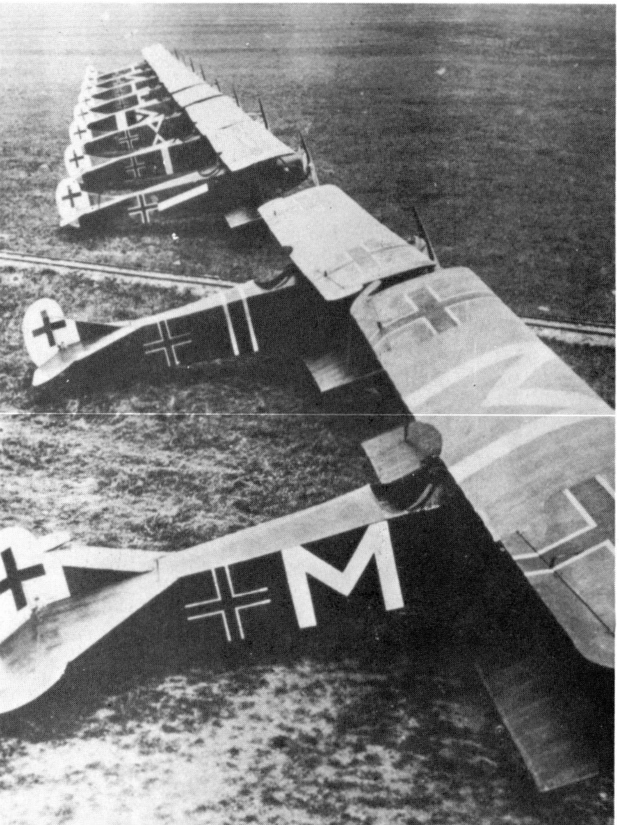

▲73   ▼74

72. *Leutnant* Karl Menckhoff, *Staffelführer* of *Jagdstaffel 72*. Having served on two-seaters on the Eastern Front as a *Vizefeldwebel* before attending the fighter schools at both Warsaw and Valenciennes, Menckhoff was assigned to *Jagdstaffel 3* in February 1917 and logged twenty victories before being commissioned and given the command of *Jagdstaffel 72*. Following his 25th victory, he was awarded the *Ordre Pour le Mérite* on 23 April 1918.

73. Fokker DVIIs of *Jagdstaffel 72* lined up at Bergnicourt aerodrome, July 1918. Menckhoff's aircraft is nearest the camera, marked on fuselage and top wing centre-section with a white 'M'. He was brought down by Lt. Walter Avery of the 95th US Aero Squadron at Chateau-Thierry on 25 July 1918 and captured, Menckhoff, with 39 victories, being the US aviator's first success in aerial combat. Menckhoff escaped from his prisoner-of-war camp on 23 August 1919 and reached Switzerland, where he eventually took up residence and became engaged in local industry.

74. Max Müller was a prewar military pilot who, after outstanding service on two-seaters in *Feldfliegerabteilung 1b*, converted to Fokker E monoplanes in May 1916. He was slow to achieve success as a fighter pilot but claimed five victories in *Jagdstaffel 2* (*Boelcke*) late in 1916 before being posted to the newly formed *Jagdstaffel 28*. His victory score now mounted steadily, and with 25 to his credit he was promoted to *Leutnant* in July 1917, being awarded the *Ordre Pour le Mérite* on 3 September. He is seen here on 21 August 1917 with Martinside Elephant 7276, his 26th victory.

75. Max Müller photographed with his Albatros DV, 1154/17, during his service with *Jagdstaffel 28*. He returned to *Jasta Boelcke* in November and scored another seven victories before being killed when he was shot down in flames when attacking an RE8 of No. 21 Squadron crewed by Captain G. Zimmer (pilot) and 2/Lt. H. Somerville (observer) on 9 January 1918. Credited with 38 victories, Müller was posthumously awarded the Military Max-Joseph Order on 7 November 1918.

75 ▶

76. Pilots of the lightweight, rotary-engined monoplanes did not always at first appreciate the inertia that the heavy, stationary-engined Albatros D type fighter biplanes possessed. Whether for this reason or because of a technical fault, *Leutnant* Max Ritter von Mulzer, who was credited with ten victories, was killed on 26 September 1916 when he crashed on a familiarization flight on Albatros DI 424/16, a machine destined for his *KEK III*.

77. *Leutnant* Ulrich Neckel came from the *Jagdstaffelschule* in Valenciennes to *Jagdstaffel 12* as a *Gefreiter* (lance corporal) in September 1917 and received rapid promotion due entirely to his air-fighting ability. He was commissioned in April 1918 and had nineteen victories by 10 July. On that day confirmation came through for a Sopwith Camel claimed on 3 July, and he celebrated in the time-honoured fashion by being photographed in front of his laurel-wreath-decorated Fokker DVII.

78. Neckel, *Staffelführer* of *Jagdstaffel 6*, with his black and white, oblique-striped Fokker DVII, complete with teddy bear mascot perched on the rear-view mirror; the colour scheme was said to put enemy pilots off their aim by creating an optical illusion. Appointed *Staffelführer* of *Jagdstaffel 19* in August 1918, he was posted to *Jagdgeschwader I* in September in command of *Jagdstaffel 6*. Neckel was awarded the *Ordre Pour le Mérite* on 8 November, with 30 victories, and died in Italy from tuberculosis on 11 May 1928.

79. An LVG CI two-seater of *II Marinefeldfliegerabteilung* at Mariakerke in Flanders in 1916. The observer (right) with binoculars and 25cm hand-held camera is *Leutnant* Theo Osterkamp, who after learning to fly at Johannisthal and taking the single-seater course at Putzig was assigned to the *Marinefeldjagdstaffel* under Sachsenberg. With the expansion of the naval landplane fighter force, Osterkamp became *Staffelführer* of *II Marinefeldjagdstaffel* and had ten victories by the end of April 1918.

78▲   79▼

▲ 80　▼ 81

82▲

80. The clean lines of the Fokker EV parasol monoplane fighter are evident in this view of Osterkamp and his machine taken in August 1918. Awarded the *Ordre Pour le Mérite* on 2 September, Osterkamp survived the war with 31 victories and served in *Kampfgeschwader Sachsenberg* on Germany's eastern borders in 1919. He remained in aviation and joined the *Luftwaffe* in 1935, formed and was *Kommodore* of *JG 51* early in the Second World War and despite his age flew Messerschmitt Bf 109s operationally, gaining six victories. He was awarded the *Ritterkreuz* in August 1940, his rank at the end of hostilities being *Generalleutnant* (Air Vice Marshal). Osterkamp died on 2 January 1975.

81. *Oberleutnant* Otto Parschau was a prewar military pilot whose experience was put to good use when he assisted Anthony Fokker in introducing the Fokker monoplane to front-line units during the summer of 1915. Following his eighth victory on 10 July 1916 he was awarded the *Ordre Pour le Mérite*, the sixth fighter pilot to be so decorated, but was mortally wounded in aerial combat eleven days later. He is seen here with his Fokker EIV, the final version of the Fokker monoplane.

82. This BE2c of No. 12 Squadron RFC, crewed by 2/Lt. N. Gordon-Smith (pilot) and 2/Lt. D. Cunningham-Reid (observer), was shot down near Brugge on 19 December 1915 by Otto Parschau (extreme right in centre group) on a Fokker monoplane as his second victory. The cumbersome BE2c was no match for the nimble, machine-gun-armed Fokker monoplane and the type figures prominently in the victory logs of early German fighter pilots.

83. *Leutnant* Fritz Pütter, *Staffelführer* of *Jagdstaffel 68*, who served on two-seaters in *Fliegerabteilung (A) 251* before going to *Jagdstaffel 9* in March 1917. Appointed to the command of *Jagdstaffel 68* following his tenth victory, Pütter was awarded the *Ordre Pour le Mérite* on 31 May 1918. On 16 July his Fokker DVII burst into flames when its phosphorous ammunition spontaneously ignited, and although Pütter landed successfully he had sustained serious burns, from which he died on 10 August. He was credited with 25 victories, including eight balloons.

◀83

45

▲ 84 ▼ 85

84. *Leutnant* Lothar Freiherr von Richthofen being assisted from the cockpit of his Albatros DIII, a machine on which he obtained 24 victories. Trained initially as an observer, Lothar served in *Kampfstaffel 23* during 1916 and after learning to fly was able to join his brother Manfred in *Jagdstaffel 11* during March 1917. His performance as an *ab initio* fighter pilot has never been equalled; he scored twenty victories in a four-week period and was awarded the *Ordre Pour le Mérite* on 4 May.

85. Lothar von Richthofen with his Fokker DrI triplane when *Staffelführer* of *Jagdstaffel 11*, March 1918. Said by contemporary pilots to have been a greater exponent of the art of air-fighting than his famous brother, he was absent from the Front for long periods because of wounds, illness and crash injuries. During the whole of his service in *Jagdstaffel 11* he undertook only 77 operational flights yet obtained 40 victories, ten of them in the first twelve days of September 1918 before wounds terminated his combat flying activities. Promoted to *Oberleutnant*, he was killed at Hamburg while carrying out a forced landing after his civil aircraft suffered engine failure on 4 July 1922.

86. A then unknown two-seater pilot in *Kampfgeschwader II*, *Leutnant* Manfred Freiherr von Richthofen was chosen by Boelcke to join him in his newly created *Jagdstaffel 2* then forming on the Somme and became one of Boelcke's best pupils, soon being entrusted with the leading of fighting formations. He is seen here, second from the right, with Kirmaier, Immelmann and Wortmann, in front of his Albatros DII at Lagnicourt aerodrome, November 1916. After obtaining sixteen victories he was awarded the *Ordre Pour le Mérite* on 12 January 1917 and three days later was given the command of *Jagdstaffel 11*. He led this unit in the best Boelcke tradition and fostered a number of highly successful air fighters like Allmenröder, Schäfer, Wolff and his own brother Lothar.

87. Manfred von Richthofen and Dutch aircraft designer Anthony Fokker sit on the rear fuselage of Lieutenant A. F. Bird's Sopwith Pup which Bird, of No. 46 Squadron RFC, deliberately steered into a tree to damage the aircraft. This was Richthofen's 61st victory and the second that he scored on the Fokker triplane. Bird was brought down near Bousbecque on 3 September 1917.

86 ▲   87 ▼

B
1795

▲ 88   ▼ 89

88. Manfred von Richthofen (centre) with the leaders of his component *Jagdstaffeln*, March 1918: (left to right) Wüsthoff (*Jasta 4*), Reinhard (*Jasta 6*), Löwenhardt (*Jasta 10*) and Lothar von Richthofen (*Jasta 11*), whose combined effort amounted to 221 victories. Reinhard, credited with twenty victories, was Manfred von Richthofen's successor as *Kommandeur* of *Jagdgeschwader I*, but only he among this group did not receive the *Ordre Pour le Mérite*: although recommended for the decoration, he was killed on a test flight in Berlin before the award could be made.

89. One of the last photographs taken of Manfred von Richthofen: while Löwenhardt watches, the *Rittmeister* plays with his dog, Moritz. He was shot down and killed on 21 April 1918 apparently by fire from the ground while following a Sopwith Camel across the lines at low altitude. On 20 May the formation that he had so successfully led was officially named *Jagdgeschwader Freiherr von Richthofen Nr. I* and at the end of the war was credited with an aggregate of 644 victories.

90. The 'Balloon Buster': *Leutnant* Fritz Röth, *Staffelführer* of *Jagdstaffel 16b* poses with his Albatros DVa. Röth flew two-seaters with *Fliegerabteilung (A) 296b* before serving in *Jagdstaffeln 34b* and *23b*. He shot down three French observation balloons during one flight in January 1918, four British balloons on one flight in April and five British balloons in May, again on one flight. Promoted to *Oberleutnant*, he was awarded the *Ordre Pour le Mérite* on 9 September.

91. *Oberleutnant* Schleich, leader of *Jagdgruppe 8b*, with *Leutnant* Kissenberth, leader of Jasta 23b (left), and *Leutnant* Röth, in front of Kissenberth's LFG Roland DVIb single-seater. Röth survived the war, having scored 28 victories that included twenty observation balloons, but he committed suicide on 31 December 1918 and thus did not live to learn of his award of the Military Max-Joseph Order on 18 May 1920.

90 ▲   91 ▼

92. The three best air-fighters in *Jagdstaffel* 5 were (left to right) *Vizefeldwebel* Fritz Rumey, Otto Könnecke and Josef Mai: all received the highest NCO award, the *Goldenen Militär-Verdienst Kreuz*, and all were promoted to *Leutnant* for bravery in the face of the enemy. Only Mai did not receive the *Ordre Pour le Mérite*, since, despite his 30 victories, the recommendation for this highest military decoration came late and hostilities ended before it could be awarded. Tis trio were responsible for the destruction of 110 Allied aircraft.

93. After flying two-seaters in various units for over eighteen months, Rumey joined *Jagdstaffel* 5 via the *Jagdstaffelschule* in Valenciennes in June 1917; commissioned one year later, he was awarded the *Ordre Pour le Mérite* on 10 July 1918 and obtained his 30th victory soon afterwards. Most of his flying was on Albatros DVs and DVas, but he also flew the Fokker DrI triplane, crashing the machine shown in the photograph when engine failure caused him to collide with a barbed-wire entanglement. Rumey was killed on 27 September when his Fokker DVII broke up in the air following a collision with a Sopwith Camel a few minutes after he scored his 45th victory.

94. *Leutnant zur See* Gottard Sachsenberg in the cockpit of Fokker EIII monoplane LF 196 attached to the naval two-seater unit *I Marinefeldfliegerabteilung* at Mariakerke in 1916. Sachsenberg learned to fly at Johannisthal while he was running an observer's course and quickly converted to single-seaters. When the landplane fighters allocated to the *Marine Korps* in Flanders were assembled into a permanent formation and named the *Marinefeldjadgstaffel* in April 1917, Sachsenberg was given the command.

95. Albatros DVa single-seat fighters of the *Marinefeldjagdgruppe* taking off from Aertrycke aerodrome, led by Sachsenberg in the machine in the foreground marked with a black and white chequered fuselage band. The naval landplane fighters were eventually formed into the *Marinefeldjagdgeschwader*, comprising *Marinefeldjagdstaffeln I* to *V* under Sachsenberg who was awarded the *Ordre Pour le Mérite* on 5 August 1918. He survived the war with 31 victories and formed and operated a 70-aircraft flying formation named *Kampfgeschwader Sachsenberg* in the fighting on Germany's eastern borders in 1919. Associated with the Junkers aircraft organization from the early 1920s, Sachsenberg died on 23 August 1961.

94▲ 95▼

96. *Leutnant* Emil Schaefer, *Staffelführer* of *Jagdstaffel 28* and seen here with his red Albatros DIII, flew with Richthofen in *Kampfgeschwader II* in Russia and by early 1917 was flying Albatros DII single-seaters in that unit, which had in the meantime returned to the Western Front. Schaefer joined *Jagdstaffel 11* in February, and such was his success that in April, with 23 victories to his credit, he was appointed to the command of *Jagdstaffel 28*. A few days later, on 30 April he was awarded the *Ordre Pour le Mérite*.

97. Schaefer's 30th and last victory: the wreckage of DH4 A7420 from No. 55 Squadron, crewed by 2/Lt. D. J. Honer and Pte. G. Cluney, brought down over Moorslede on 4 June 1917. Schaefer was shot down and killed the following day by an FE2d of No. 20 Squadron flown by Lt. H. L. Satchell and 2/Lt. T. Lewis.

▲96   ▼97

98. *Oberleutnant* Eduard Schleich with his Albatros CI from *Feldfliegerabteilung 2b*, early in 1916. A professional soldier, by the end of 1917 he had scored 25 victories as the *Staffelführer* of *Jagdstaffel 21*, receiving the *Ordre Pour le Mérite* on 4 December. In 1918, after leading *Jagdstaffel 32b* and *Jagdgruppe 8b*, he was promoted to *Hauptmann* and became the *Kommandeur* of *Jagdgeschwader 4b*, comprising *Jagdstaffeln 23b, 32b, 34b* and *35b*.

99. The Black Knight. Hauptmann Eduard Ritter von Schleich received the Military Max-Joseph Order on 6 July 1918 and flew both his Albatros DVa and Fokker DVII painted black. He was the proud possessor of a British leather flying coat, a garment much coveted by the German airmen, and he is seen here beside his Albatros DVa. Note the signal cartridges in the cockpit rack, the rear-view mirror and the tubular gun-sight. Von Schleich survived the war having scored 35 victories and was active in promoting airmindedness amongst the Hitler Youth in the 1930s. He died in Munich on 15 November 1947.

98 ▲ 99 ▼

▲ 100 ▼101　　　　　▼102

100. *Leutnant* Karl Thom of *Jagdstaffel 21* in his Fokker DVII; the aircraft carries his personal 'T' marking and the black and white fuselage bands denoting his unit. The Fokker DVII, immensely strong, highly manoeuvrable, and with its cantilever wings devoid of bracing wires, was the finest fighter of the war. The BMW-powered version was capable of 122mph and could climb to 20,000ft in 21 minutes. Over 800 machines of this type were with the front-line units by the end of August 1918.

101. Thom converted to single-seaters at Valenciennes and joined *Jagdstaffel 21* as a *Vizefeldwebel* in May 1917. In October, with twelve victories to his credit, he was awarded the *Goldenen Militär-Verdienst Kreuz*. On three occasions he brought down three enemy aircraft in one day, and was badly wounded in August 1918. Promoted to *Leutnant*, he was awarded the *Ordre Pour le Mérite* on 1 November and was credited with 27 victories. To prevent his beloved Fokker DVII from being delivered to the Allies after the Armistice he deliberately wrote it off in a crash landing and was himself badly injured. A staunch supporter of National Socialism, he held high office in Eastern Germany and is presumed not to have survived the Second World War.

102. *Vizefeldwebel* Emil Thuy, a two-seater pilot in *Feldfliegerabteilung 53*, poses with the *Ehrenbecher 'Dem Sieger im Luftkampf'* awarded for his first victory on 8 September 1915. The *Ehrenbecher*, finely made from high-quality silver, was sponsored by rich industrialists and was presented at this time to every air fighter following his first victory. As the war continued the *Ehrenbecher* was made from lower grade material and a number of victories were then required before pilots could qualify for its award.

103. Promoted to *Leutnant*, Thuy served in *Jagdstaffel 21* from its formation at the end of 1916 and, with fifteen victories, he was given the command of *Jagdstaffel 28* at the end of September 1917. When he was awarded the *Ordre Pour le Mérite* on 30 June 1918 his score stood at 23, and this increased to 32 by the Armistice. After the war he was active in aviation technical circles until he met his death in a flying accident on 11 June 1930 near Smolensk in Russia.

103▶

104. *Oberleutnant* Adolf Ritter von Tutschek (left) with his observer *Leutnant* Freiherr von Stein of *Feldfliegerabteilung 6b* seen with their Albatros CVII after a forced landing following an air combat on 26 December 1916. Although witnesses were obtained for two enemy aircraft shot down, the victories were not officially confirmed. The Albatros two-seater, with rudder controls shot away, narrowly missed some high-tension cables and barbed wire entanglements, and carried away two field telegraph wires, the remnants of which can be seen wrapped around the propeller spinner.

105. After three months in *Jagdstaffel Boelcke*, von Tutschek was given the command of *Jagdstaffel 12* in April 1917. He was awarded the *Ordre Pour le Mérite* on 7 August following his 21st victory but was severely wounded in the right shoulder four days later. When *Jagdgeschwader II*, comprising *Jagdstaffeln 12, 13, 15* and *19*, was formed in February 1918, von Tutschek, in the meantime promoted to *Hauptmann*, became its *Kommandeur*. He is shown here taking off from Toulis aerodrome in his Fokker DrI, flying leader's wing-tip streamers. Credited with 27 victories, he was killed in aerial combat on 15 March 1918.

106. *Vizefeldwebel* Ernst Udet (left) and *Vizefeldwebel* Weingärtner, with a Fokker EIII of *Kampfeinsitzer Kommando Habsheim*, March 1916. Udet took private flying lessons early in 1915 to gain direct entry to the air service, and after flying two-seaters for four months converted to Fokker E monoplanes in November. He scored his first victory in March 1916 and by the end of the year had three victories. He was commissioned in January 1917, serving at the time with *Jagdstaffel 15*, which had been formed out of the *KEK Habsheim*.

106▶

▲ 104 ▼ 105

107. Udet, with eight victories, became the *Staffelführer* of *Jagdstaffel 37* in September 1917, his black-fuselage Albatros DVa being marked with 'LO' as his personal marking. In March 1918, with 20 victories to his credit, he joined *JG I* and was at first acting *Staffelführer* of *Jagdstaffel 11* and later *Staffelführer* of *Jagdstaffel 4*. When Udet was awarded the *Ordre Pour le Mérite* on 9 April his score stood at 23 victories, and this had increased to 35 when on 28 June he was shot down by an alert observer in a French Breguet 14 and saved his life by jumping by parachute from his crippled Fokker DVII.

108. Promoted to *Oberleutnant* in September, Udet was, at the time of the Armistice, the highest-scoring surviving German fighter pilot, with 62 victories. Devoted to aviation, he formed his own aircraft manufacturing company in 1922, but soon concentrated on stunt flying and was immensely popular with the crowds who flocked to see him fly. He reluctantly joined the *Luftwaffe* in 1935. He hated 'flying a desk', and, blamed for certain *Luftwaffe* shortcomings, he committed suicide on 17 November 1941. He held the rank of *Generaloberst* (Air Chief Marshal).

▲ 107 ▼ 108

109. A two-seater crew from *Feldfliegerabteilung 23* at Roupy in 1916 with their Albatros BI. The pilot (left) is *Vizefeldwebel* Josef Veltjens, who after being commissioned and converting to single-seaters at Paderborn served under Berthold in *Jagdstaffeln 14* and *18*. He had twelve victories when, in May 1918, he became the *Staffelführer* of *Jagdstaffel 15*. One of his pilots in this unit was the observer seen with him here, *Leutnant* Joachim von Ziegesar.

110. Veltjens in his 'Indian arrow' marked Albatros DV when a member of *Jagdstaffel 18*. Awarded the *Ordre Pour le Mérite* on 16 August 1918 (the day that he brought down his 24th victory), he was finally credited with 35 victories. Veltjens served again in the new *Luftwaffe* with the rank of *Oberst* (Group Captain) but was killed on 6 October 1943 when his Junkers Ju 52/3m transport was shot down over Yugoslavia by partisans.

109▲ 110▼

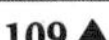

▲ 111   ▼ 112

The photograph at top shows aircraft number **113▲**

111. *Leutnant* Werner Voss of *Jagdstaffel Boelcke* , his Albatros DIII
decorated with his personal insignia. Voss flew two-seaters with
Kampfstaffel 20 at Verdun and on the Somme before joining *Jagdstaffel
2* in November 1916, scoring 27 victories with the unit. He was
decorated with the *Ordre Pour le Mérite* on 8 April 1917. After service in
Jagdstaffel 5 and *14* this fearless fighter was made *Staffelführer* of
Jagdstaffel 10 in July and achieved 48 victories before he was killed in
action.

112. On 23 September 1917 Voss in this Fokker FI triplane (103/17)
fought a single-handed combat lasting ten minutes against seven SE5a
aircraft from No. 56 Squadron flown by some of the finest pilots in the
RFC. He hit all their machines in turn, but possibly the sustained flick
manoeuvres that he used overstressed his controls, or else he ran out of
fuel: in any event, unable to avoid 2/Lt. Rhys-David's fire, he was shot
down and killed. McCudden, who took part in the fight later wrote 'As
long as I live I shall never forget my admiration for that German pilot . . .
His flying was wonderful, his courage magnificent . . .'

113. Flying a Walfisch two-seater in *Feldfliegerabteilung 62*,
Vizefeldwebel Rudolf Windisch landed his observer with demolition
charges 85km behind the Russian lines on 2 October 1916 to blow up
the Rowno–Brody railway line, returning the following day to pick him
up. Decorated for this feat, he was promoted to *Leutnant*, converted to
single-seaters early in 1917 and served in *Jagdstaffeln 32* and *50*. He had
obtained eight victories when he was appointed to *Jagdstaffel 66* as
Staffelführer in January 1918.

114. Windisch with his Spad 7 on the aerodrome at Norman le Wast;
the aircraft was one of eight Spads in use by the Germans at the time.
Windisch, with 22 victories, was brought down behind the French lines
on 27 May and was reported to be a prisoner-of-war; a few days later
advancing German troops recovered his Fokker DVII, which was not
badly damaged. The award of the *Ordre Pour le Mérite* was made to
Windisch on 6 June, and since he was not present to receive this
personally it was given into the care of *Kogenluft* (General in command
of the air service) ten days later. However, no further news of Windisch
was ever heard and his disappearance remains a mystery.

◄114

▲115 ▼116

115. *Leutnant* Kurt Wintgens learned to fly at the Fokker school at Schwerin early in 1915, and, being instructed in Fokker techniques and in the handling of rotary engines, he was a natural choice to fly the early Fokker E monoplanes. There is strong evidence to suggest that he fought the first successful combat on the type when, as a member of *Feldfliegerabteilung 6b*, he forced a French Morane Parasol to land east of Lunéville on 1 July 1915. He is seen here in February 1916 with one of the first Fokker EIV monoplanes, 124/15.

116. Wintgens, seen here in the cockpit of his Halberstadt DII, was the third fighter pilot to be decorated with the *Ordre Pour le Mérite*, which he received on 1 July 1916 following his eighth victory. Belonging to *Feldfliegerabteilung 67* in 1916, he was attached to various single-seater formations, including *Kampfstaffel Falkenhausen* and *Kampfeinsitzer Kommando Vaux*. When he was killed on 25 September 1916 he was serving with *Jagdstaffel 1* and had nineteen victories.

117. *Leutnant* Kurt Wolff with his Halberstadt DV. Wolff served in *Kampfstaffel 40* before joining *Jagdstaffel 11* in November 1916. He scored 22 victories during April 1917 and was awarded the *Ordre Pour le Mérite* on 5 May. He was killed on 15 September flying one of the early Fokker triplanes as *Staffelführer* of *Jagdstaffel 11*, having been credited with 33 victories.

118. This FE8 6456 of No. 40 Squadron RFC, was usually flown by Lt. Walder, but on 9 March 1917 Lt. Shepherd was at the controls when during an air-fight with *Jagdstaffel 11* he was shot down near Annay on the Lens–Carvin road by Kurt Wolff, whose second victory this was.

117▲

118▼

119. Kurt Wüsthoff had just turned seventeen years of age when he learned to fly. He served in *Kampfgeschwader I* as a *Vizefeldwebel* before joining *Jagdstaffel 4* in June 1917. Promoted to *Leutnant* in July, he was awarded the *Ordre Pour le Mérite* on 22 November with 26 victories to his credit. He is seen here with Sub-Lt. Wilford's Sopwith Triplane (N5429) from No. 1 Squadron RNAS, which he brought down on 13 September as his fifteenth victory.

120. When Wüsthoff, *Staffelführer* of *Jagdstaffel 4*, returned to the Front in June 1918 following a three-month absence due to sickness, he was assigned to *Jagdstaffel 15* in *Jagdgeschwader II* but was shot down and taken prisoner on his first operational flight with that unit. Flying *Leutnant* Georg von Hantelmann's red and blue Fokker DVII on 17 June 1918, he fell victim to a flight of SE5as from No. 24 Squadron. Wüsthoff died on 23 July 1926 from injuries received when he crashed during an air display at Dresden.

▲119 ▼120